Wouldn't You Rather Be Laughing:

Comedy Therapies for Sad People

Mudditors of MuddyUm

Garden of Neuro

GARDEN OF NEURO
INSTITUTE

ISBN Paperback 979-8-9851332-3-3
November 2022

Editing: Toni Crowe, Gary Chapin, Andrew Rodwin
Cover: Sara Zadrima
Formatting: Help Just One
Print Publishing Consultation by Prolific Pulse Press
LLC

Dedication

This book is dedicated to Roger Rabbit, who said, "Sometimes a laugh is the most important thing we have." A laugh can lift our spirits, improve our health, and even get us through sex gone awry. A laugh can get us through bad times and even help topple tyrants. Laughter can even win love itself. Who can forget Jessica Rabbit? When asked what she saw in that lunatic, she needed only four words: "He makes me laugh."

"Everything is funny, as long as it's happening to somebody else."

— Will Rogers

Table of Funtents

Foreplay

Granny Mary

Granny Mary began writing an advice column for MuddyUm in 2021. She died in 1996.

This is hard, writing a foreword to this anthology. The weight of responsibility. I wasn't prepared for the sense of gravitas it would inspire in my cold, dead heart.

My regular work, as you well know, is answering questions of the 'lorn— lovelorn, worklorn, buttlorn. People who write to me are desperate (or sanguine), young (or old), and at a crossroads (or in a cul-de-sac). Thus, I feel no compunction taking their concerns lightly, mocking them, piling on the absurdity, misinterpreting them on purpose, distracting myself with comic sequiturs, and sacrificing their goodwill to the Gods of comedy. The image of them reading my columns with hurt little faces makes my already brilliant comic writing that much more brilliant. If only I could share that joy with you.

It's not like that when you're writing a foreword. You have to take it very seriously. The success or failure of the entire venture rests on the ability of your words to seduce, persuade, and ensorcell innocent readers into the Pages of COMEDY! And when you've got writing as good as this—to know all of this talent will wither past

its sell-by date for lack of a good foreword? That's rough.

If I weren't already dead, the anxiety would kill me.

So, let me state the obvious. This anthology is good. Very good. I haven't read an anthology with a collection of talent like this in hours. It stands on the peak (of what? I don't know) and is sine qua only a very few things.

The abundance of comedy in these pages will leave your pants wet. It's a *shplotz*. A *shplotz* of comedy. (**Editor's Note:** *shplotz* is a fake Yiddish word that means "fifteen of something." You have a dozen, 12, a *shplotz*, 15, a gross, 144, and a *horkleshplotz,* 225. The *horkleshplotz* was used almost exclusively to schedule deliveries in "the old country," where they broke their day up into shleps, *shplotzen,* and *horkleshplotzen.* Let me tell you when you break a day up into 225 shleps, which may or may not be evenly spaced, you need all the scheduling help you can get. Back to Granny.)

There's something in this book for everybody, and everything is here for somebody. Whether it's Paul collapsing a lung, or Carol finding the clitoris (on a dolphin), or Andrew's astute, obtuse, and acute statistical political ramblings (comedy!), you will find joy in these pages.

Think of it this way. The entire goddamn world is going to shit, and you are reading a foreword written by a dead woman who was recently made famous for—get this—blowing her nose into dirty underwear.

Wouldn't you rather be laughing?

—*Granny Mary*

Acknowledgments

It has been a trip working with the Mudditors of MuddyUm putting together this Anthology. I am a Mudditor. Mudditors are the volunteer editors of MuddyUm. If you can wrap your mind around this, fourteen editors are working to share whatever knowledge we have with our MuddyUm writers to publish stories daily.

When I volunteered to work on our MuddyUm Anthology, I knew exactly how much work it was, but I counted on the fact that our editorial team steps up to do what must be done. And we did. There is no way this Anthology would have come together without the efforts of Gary Chapin and Andrew Rodwin.

Gary was a marvelous gatekeeper. Sincere, gentle with the writers, reading their submissions and responding immediately to sometimes ridiculous requests. We had one writer change their anthology story three times. Gary did not fly to their home and smack them in the head. Instead, he patiently read the inputs and provided me with the ultimate result. He shepherded the book sections like they were little lambs in need of protection.

Andrew played a crucial role in technical support. Since we started with fifteen separate stories and not a manuscript, all the pieces needed to be gathered from the humorists. There were things that each of our writers

needed to learn so that we would have a collaborative quality product. Andrew provided that information. He squeezed various pieces of information required for the stories out of the editors, gathered the links, made opinion polls, and offered many ways for every editor to take part.
Without Gary and Andrew, this book would have been an impossible task. Thank you.

Enjoy the book. The Mudditors are hilarious.

Toni Crowe
Editor
Tampa, Florida, September 2022

Introduction

What you hold in your hands is not just a collection of funny stories. What you have is a key, one of many, to unlock a path to healing. Healing may be too strong of a word. Let's just say, a number of years ago, I needed a new direction. And after medical recommendations and making some big decisions for myself, I discovered I needed to laugh more. I wasn't really laughing at all, so any amount would have been an improvement.

The journey through the things that take away our joy is not the same for everyone, yet at some point in the process, we all can begin to smile again. It starts small and grows until one day, we find ourselves laughing out loud, in public.

But what happens when the 'public' is taken away? In 2020, I was ready to step onto a stage and share the humor I'd found on the other side of my personal darkness. Then everything, for everyone, changed. And for some magical, mystical reason, the choices I made during this moment changed everything. Not just for me, but for a group of people who might never have met, had the whole world not stopped spinning because of a pandemic.

In the subsequent months, and now years that followed, we have grown into a family. It's hard to imagine life without them. I feel I know them on a deeper level than the 'real' people who surround me in daily life, even though the majority of us have not met in person. This has not stopped us from creating joy on every level possible. Our editorial meetings are so much fun, we record them as evidence of how hilarious we are.

You are now holding all the healing, growth, and pure joy created by one massively wonderful collaborative project, put together by people around the world who were meant to meet. Maybe the world stopped just so our paths would cross and this book would be created to help others' laugh—because it's the sign you, we, and I, have all made it to the other side.

The scones are really good here. We're always making more.

They'll be fresh when you arrive. ;)

Susan Brearley
Poughkeepsie, New York, July 2022

Chapter 1

Why We Live in a World Dominated by Men : Men seem to be at the beginning of everything

Anu Anniah

Author | Writer | Poet. Bangalore, India. Sometimes, I show you life through a 'fun' filter. Sometimes life is 'laid bare.' anuanniahwrites.in/

I know if it is a sheer coincidence that men are responsible for starting all kinds of things on Earth. I mean, there is war and such like, but I am not talking about that … at least not in this post.

Simple things — things which you would think men have no connection with and yet there they are right at the beginning. Don't agree? Stay with me for just a little bit, please.

Consider the word '*men.*' A harmless three-letter word to indicate roughly 50% of the human population.

Add a small 'u' at the end. What do you have? A list of things to eat. I mean what do men have to do with what anyone eats? Why should menu start with men?

The one word that begins with *men* and probably makes sense in an abstract way is *mental*. I refuse to state anything else here.

What about *mentor*, I ask? Was the first person who ever mentored anyone a man? Is that it? Is that how words are formed now? Just for once, could they not have said *womentor?*

Take *menthol.* What is the deal here? Only men can be cool, huh?

I mean, it is almost as if I cannot *mention* anything without men being called upon.

How about this one? *Menacing!* Dangerous, threatening!

The worst of them is *meningitis.* What? Only men have brains and therefore can get diseases related to the brain? Is that the message here?

I am not saying every word that begins with men should be modified to begin with women. I am not even going to remotely suggest that the words be gender-neutral and start with *person.*

Persontor, personthol, and *personu* would sound pretty weird!

I was proceeding along on this train of thought and collecting words for the case when suddenly two words threw me completely. I can't even contemplate why and who decided these words.

Menstruation and *menopause*. Why are men involved in this?!! What is their role? What is their contribution? Did they help start our periods? Do they help us end it? Do they share the load at any point during the month-on-month year-after-year saga? How would that go?

Wife: Honey, I am really busy at work this month and there is a lot of business travel coming up. Can you handle my menstruation just for this month?

Husband: Sure thing. Let me just nip out to the store and get some manpads.

Not happening, right? It was nice to dream just for a little bit.

Who creates these words? Who writes the *dictionary* (no, no we will not digress and examine the starting letters of this word)? What were they thinking? I really want to ask the folks that came up with *menstruation*. Bad enough it is a pain. Worse, it is confusing to pronounce what with the math folks having something called *mensuration!* Women can't measure or what?

I'm telling you, ladies! This is just the tip of the iceberg. Way back in time, I think all the men got together in a huddle and decided to take over the world from us women. And one of the ways they listed was to keep us women spellbound!

I think spellings are a subtle way of establishing their dominance. It is subliminal messaging. They thought we wouldn't notice. We are onto it now though. Just don't *womention* it to them.

Chapter 2

Ladies, Get Yours Today: And everyday

Nanci Arvizu

Write Your Story Speak Your Truth Play Your Game.
Intentionally, relentlessly, pursue your passion.
nanciwrites.substack.com

Ladies. Let's Talk.

D you dream of a destressed life? Days feeling less on edge, when the 'dreaded 11s' don't have a reason to form because you started your morning, and every morning, getting off on the right foot?

Having trouble finding satisfaction throughout your busy day? Are you, or your partner, too tired to take care of your business in the bedroom?

Ready to remodel?

Introducing the Ultimate Problematic Truncheon Replacement System. It not only takes care of every woman's daily care needs, but it also looks stunning in the bathroom.

The UTR-1000 Showerhead by H2ooooo, that also

brought half the world's population the best-selling Womxn Water, SuidaeSkaSti Oils, providing more than just pleasure: A Purpose.

Forged from the finest metal peoplekind has ever produced, the smooth glistening handle is designed to fit every hand, from the delicate jewel clutcher to the mighty grip of self-knowledge, the UTR-1000 is the first of its kind to truly turn shower and/or bath time into specific 'You' time.

With 12 head settings to deliver jets of pulsating water exactly where *you* know you need, the UTR-1000 promises to provide the healing benefits of personal care all women desire and deserve. Just pure, quiet (or not, music is always good too) time to discover and enjoy the personal pleasures of the UTR-1000.

We are so sure you will fall in love with the UTR-1000 we're offering rebates to help offset the new, higher water bills you're sure to have as you explore all the ways the UTR-1000 can improve your overall well-being because while sex sells, the UTR-1000 by H2ooooo delivers results. And unlike pharmaceuticals, on-demand, and without the drama.

But Wait! There's More!

Order yours within the next thirty minutes and we'll throw in the Ultimate in Female Personal Water Care, the *Hit Me With Your Best Shot Strap-On,* a value of unimaginable pleasure peaks, so the operator will have to explain this extra perk when you call to order.

Don't Wait! Get Yours Today.

And Every Day.
The UTR-1000, the Ultimate Problematic Truncheon
Replacement System.

Chapter 3

New Study Shows Negative Correlation Between Eating Frogs and Productivity : Business executives rethinking strategy

Susan Brearley

Susan Brearley
EIC-MuddyUm-Contemplate-Garden of Neuro.20X
Medium top writer. Writing comedy since Age 3.
Founder, Garden of Neuro. Edited once by Ev Wiliams.
He found a typo. gardenofneuroleadership.com/

WASHINGTON, DC Jan 2021 —

In a groundbreaking study, scientists discovered that eating frogs definitely will not lead to a successful or more productive life.

In an interview, the lead biochemist Ph.D. student Alfred B. Oldman shared, "Our hypothesis came to us in a late night working session over pizza, where our professor and cohort of grad students were talking about this book that purportedly has sold over 2 million copies."

The first version, the 'green book' — written for business audiences — sold fewer. The book apparently claims that eating frogs will lead to greater success in life by helping people to stop procrastinating. Some among us are avid gardeners and frogophiles and were upset that people actually believed in this nonsense. In that moment, the plan to develop a study was born."

In a longitudinal study conducted over the past 4 years, involving 50 of the largest cities in the United States, and volunteers aged 25 through 80, located through local Craig's Lists advertisements, a broad sampling of green frog varieties were crushed and added to the diets of the volunteers. None of the volunteers knew which type of frog they were ingesting, or in what breakfast recipes the frogs would be included in, to prevent menu item bias. Meals with frog ingredients, and without frog ingredients, were measured across short and long-term duration for exposure. Only breakfasts were served, consistent with book instructions to "eat the frog, first thing in the day."

A series of standard cognitive, physiological, MRI and CT brain scans were conducted with participants. Across every age group and demographic except one, there were no measurable performance enhancements, thereby debunking the idea that eating frogs is in any way a performance enhancement or helps lead one to eliminate procrastination. In fact, in the 60–80 demographic group, data indicated that procrastination was increased. Arrival times to the breakfast halls were significantly decreased from the first 3 years of the study. Older volunteers frequently arrived late, or not at all, through much of 2020.

The one group that did show a measurable difference in performance came to be known as TNT20. This hybrid group consumed a frog variety that contained poison dart frog. They all died.

Oldman continued, "Surprisingly, we only purchased non-toxic green frogs for the study, to be faithful to the spirit of the book. We later discovered that our vendor allowed the poison dart frogs to be shipped in the same box with the green frogs. Initially, there was no way we could find out which frogs got consumed by who, due to the depth of the study parameters. We performed autopsies showing the toxin in the systems of those volunteers who died, which is what signaled us to call the vendor. The bodies just kept dropping. You know, we would have tested on rats, but then we wouldn't have been able to do the cognitive tests required to prove our hypothesis —"

"That eating frogs definitely does not help performance. In fact, in some cases, it's downright deadly."

The autopsies were performed at no charge to the families of the deceased volunteers.
The United States Department of Health and Human Services, which funded the study, had no comment.

Chapter 4

How to Blow Your Nose into Dirty Underwear : Follow my grandmother's example

Gary Chapin

All-time Top Writer in Accordions. I write. I have always written. I play accordion. I have an extraordinary ability to be fascinated by things.
garyparkerchapin.medium.com

I ask you to set aside your naiveté or world-weariness. I ask you to understand that however long or well you've been blowing your nose into dirty underwear — whether it's your first time or 10,000th — you can always improve the efficiency, artfulness, and elan of your approach. Certainly, you can learn from my grandmother,

Grandma Mary

I discovered my grandmother's mastery of blowing her nose into dirty underwear late in her life. It seems obvious, now, but had never come up. She was born British in 1920 and grew up in Japan as daughter of the consulate to the Emperor's Court . Of course, she could blow her nose into dirty underwear with style and grace.

One morning shortly after the turn of the millennium, I

picked her up at the Methodist Assisted Living facility in Ocean Grove, NJ. She still wasn't out of bed. We did all the "hello, Grandma" stuff and agreed that the plan was breakfast and then a walk on the beach. She sat up on the edge of her bed and made snuffling noises.

Pay careful attention to this next part.

She reaches out with her left hand to a pile of laundry on the floor. Picks up an article. Sets it back. Picks up another. No. Not that one. Picks up a third. It's a pair of white, cotton, capacious old lady underwear. She pulls it to her face and blows her nose into it.

It was glorious. Not a delicate expulsion of dried, night-time mucus, but a fully sounded, viscous note of victory, full of music and matter. Someone clearing out a shallow septic tank would not have heard noise as angelic as this. She paused, looking almost beatific, opening up the wadded cloth and examining. I could see nothing but the aura of greens and yellows, but she was satisfied. She tossed the underwear back into the laundry pile.
I stood there in awe of the aged ancestor. "Rock on, Old Lady," I muttered.

What do we learn from this?

Examine the story and you will find all the clues you need to be blowing your nose into dirty underwear in a way that improves your quality of life.

The laundry pile is at hand. My grandmother did not have to go searching for the dirty underwear. The pile was right there. Her left arm reached out in a well-practiced manner. She wasn't groping around like some noob.

She shows discernment. When you are on the run from hired assassins, you never take the first Uber that shows up, or even the second. When you are blowing your nose into dirty underwear you should only in the rarest instance settle for the first pair your hand falls upon. If the underwear is too thin, the snot will filter through like nascent cheese through a cloth. If too rough — especially on a delicate old nose like my grandmother's — chafing might occur. If there are skid marks, then —

There were no skid marks! I'm not going to embarrass the memory of my grandmother by talking about her skid marks, and I resent you for expecting me to do so.

She appreciated the moment. Notice the pause. The euphoria of one's head and septum being flushed out. Blowing your nose into dirty underwear is not a matter of utility. It's an experience both pragmatic, aesthetic, and spiritual.

She appreciated the product. Who can say what she saw written there in her snot, like prophecies in tea leaves? Was it the fecund, variable protoplasm of swamp life? Or the shimmering excellence of the Aurora Borealis? Or the tannic, synesthetic bite of the driest red wine? Whichever. It affected her. I could tell.

She did not dwell on it. The dirty underwear is tossed back in the pile, the snot to be washed away as if to nothing. Like a Buddhist sand painting destined to be obliterated by the wind, blowing your nose into dirty underwear reminds us that every moment exists only to be immediately overwritten by the next. All we have is that moment.

Carpe subvestimenta.

Chapter 5

I Explain to a GenZer That There Were Once Only Three TV Networks : They are still trying to process the concept

Betsy Denson

Medium Top Writer (x7). Freelancer for hire. Always looking for the interesting. Twitter: @BetsyDenson Facebook: @BetsyDensonWriter. betsydenson.medium.com

"I just finished the second season of Emily in Paris and there is literally nothing else to watch."

"That's because you never put down your laptop. I'd like to see how you would have survived before streaming."

"What do you mean before streaming?"

"Before you could watch anything at any time — before cable even — you just took what the Big Three offered you."

"The big three?"

"ABC, NBC, and CBS. There were three networks. That was it."

"It for what?"

"It for what you could watch. There were three channels. Oh, yea, and PBS. *For Sesame Street. "*

"Wait a second — what about Netflix? Apple TV? Hulu? There had to have been Disney, right? I mean Disney's like, eternal."

"There was Disney but it wasn't its own platform. There was The Wonderful World of Disney on CBS. That's where I saw Parent Trap and Escape to Witch Mountain. "

"Just how old is Lindsay Lohan anyway?"

"I mean the original Parent Trap with Hayley Mills. We sat on our mustard yellow sofa and watched it on our 100-pound television while we ate apples and cheese and crackers. When the show was over, we walked to the set to turn it off. "

"What about the remote control?"

"Those came later. "

"Was this like in WWII times?"

"The 1970s and 1980s. "

"So, no?"

"No."

"What was even on then? Like old movies and cooking shows and Hee Haw?"

"How do you even know what Hee Haw is?"

"TikTok."

"Of course — well there were a lot of other shows too. Happy Days and Simon & Simon and Magnum P.I. and Cheers. You know Woody Harrelson, right? He was in Cheers."

"Sure. He was a child actor, like Selena Gomez?"

"Not really. But it's relative."

"How'd you even know when your show was on anyway?"

"Oh, you knew, and if you didn't it was in the TV Guide. Which was a magazine. On paper. It was in the bathroom with the Reader's Digest. On Friday night it was Dallas. On Saturday it was the Love Boat followed by Fantasy Island. When Roots aired as a mini-series they did an episode every night for over a week. More than half the US population watched it."

"What's Roots?"

"It was originally a book by Alex Haley. A reimagining

of his African ancestors from Colonial times through the Civil War."

"Oh yeah, I think I saw the remake with Jamie Foxx. Tarantino did it?"

"Nope."

"Wait, did you say there were three networks?"

"Three main ones, yes."

"No FOX News? What did every barbershop in America put on TV then?"

"CNN I suppose. They came first. And there was WGN out of Chicago. I used to think the Cubs were the only baseball team around. Now there's a slew of them. 57 channels and nothing on."

"57 channels. That's a song. The Stones did it, right?"

"Close enough."

Chapter 6

Sex Education Tip — Keep Your Knees Together and Wear Clean Underwear : Grandfather Iron Jaw

Toni Crowe

10X Top Writer. Sarcastic escaped executive. Best-selling author of six books. Writes whatever she wants. Nerd Engineer. Twitter: @crowe
tonicrowewriter.medium.com/

The Second Grandfather

My grandmother married her second husband in her late fifties. He was the exact opposite of her first husband. He was a short stature, dark-skinned man — as honest as they came. Grandfather Iron Jaw's job was to pick up tables and chairs with his teeth for entertainment in bars and clubs. He took his orders from Grandma.

Iron Jaw seldom spoke to any of the grandchildren. Oh, he was in the house, often chuckling at our antics but did he tell us to stop? Nope. Did he tell us to go? Nope. If someone started playing with matches, Grandpa might get up out of his recliner. He would only intercede if we were going to break something of grandmother's.

Grandfather Iron Jaw once watched us play jumping

over Grandma's couch. Two of us hurt our knees because the couch was too high for kids to jump over but since we were not landing on the couch, he did not care. He told us not to bleed on the furniture.

The Birds and the Bees Talk

I remember the one time he gave me advice. My mother asked my grandmother to discuss the birds and the bees with me. Note my grandmother talked to me for twenty minutes, and when she finished, I did not know what she was talking about. I knew what birds and bees were. Was she going to take me to the local park to see some?

Grandmother then called Grandfather Iron Jaw over to finish the conversation from a man's perspective.
I will never forget what Grandfather Iron Jaw solemnly told me as he looked into my eyes. "Keep your knees together and always wear clean underwear," was the gist of his sexual advice to me.

Alrighty then. He looked at me and asked if I understood. I told him "Yes," although I did not. Grandmother was pleased. She turned and kissed him on the cheek. I stood there perplexed. I decided I would always wear clean underwear, start feeding the birds at the park regularly and stop shaking flowers when bees were on them.

Clean Panties Cure-All

My mother would kill anyone in our home trying to wear dirty or torn underwear because if you got into an accident wearing raggedy, dirty underwear, "they" would call your mother. You did not want "they" snitching on you. Our mother would be heartbroken. Now it turned out Grandfather Iron Jaw would be right there with her berating us if our panties and tee shirts were not clean. Who knew?

I will admit that, even now, I often carry an extra pair of clean panties in my bag when I'm traveling. Putting on a pair of clean panties has helped me out in tough times when there was no one to bolster my spirits when I was working in foreign lands. After traveling many hours and often heading directly into business meetings upon landing, those panties helped center me for what I needed to accomplish.

Thank you, Grandfather Iron Jaw, for that advice.

Chapter 7

My Unfavorite Things: Thank you, Julie Andrews

Holly J See

Excellent at Wordle & Sedecordle (I quit Octordle, in protest). Editor fairy & MuddyUm co-editor. Former editor at a national healthcare consulting firm. seethings99.medium.com/

Song parodies are fun to write! This is a takeoff on "My Favorite Things," a show tune from the 1959 Rodgers and Hammerstein musical, later sung by Julie Andrews in a movie classic — The Sound of Music. I sang it many times as a kid, and people still enjoy singing it in the 21st century, so you're likely familiar with the tune"

Killing of spiders and tormenting kittens
Flouting of laws whether known or unwritten
Washing a toddler covered in poo:
These are some things that I don't want to do

Puffing up proudly because I'm the greatest
Following fashion — I must have the latest
Tweeting my thoughts as if I have a clue:
These are some things that I can't or won't do

Wearing white dresses while eating spaghetti
Scaling Mount Everest in search of a yeti
Boldly displaying my F-you tattoo:
These are some things that I just wouldn't do

When the sh*t hits
And we're all screwed
And I'm feeling sad
*I simply recall what I know I **can** do:*
And then I don't feel so bad

Eating dill pickles and extra-hot hot sauce
Getting up early and being the big boss
Happily living with walls painted blue:
These are some things that I don't want to do

Up on the rooftop, I'm replacing shingles
Putting on makeup to hide all my wrinkles
Bragging that I'm so much better than you:
These are some things that I can't or won't do

Begging for money, heedless of expenses
Cheating on hubby with no consequences
Smoking fat seegars and then sniffing glue:
These are some things that I just wouldn't do

When the sh*t hits
And we're all screwed
And I'm feeling sad
I simply recall what I know I can do:
And then I don't feel so bad

There are so many things that I just wouldn't, couldn't, or prefer not to do. But lots more that I would, could, and do!

Epigraph 2

"You think therapy is fun. Try writing comedy."

— Amy Sea

Chapter 8

All Things Must Collapse : No not my pelvic floor — but I did learn to kegel

BOFace aka Monroe Baskerville

No woman ever murdered her husband while he was washing the dishes.
quasimodo.substack.com

During that magical time when I had a gorgeous body — the result of performing, on a daily basis, such physical labor as manually unloading steel bar stock from trucks — I noticed one day that the removal of a single 1" diameter bar had me slumped on a stack of pallets, gasping for breath. Must be the flu, I thought. I excused myself, drove home, and collapsed.

Awakening a few hours later and thinking, hmm, I don't feel bad at all, I make a move to rise from my mattress-on-the-floor.

Big mistake. A two-by-four launched by some invisible demonic hand slams into my chest, reeling me back to a prone position. Was I having a heart attack? Dying? Already dead, and this is Hell? *What the mother fuck! I'm only 36!*

Let's try this again. *Care-full-yyy* — OK, I'm standing. Can I drive? The hospital isn't far.

Fffuuuccckkkk! Collapsing into a chair, I call out to my roommate Ken.

"What's up? You look like shit!"

"Thanks. Could you take me to Good Samaritan?" I wheeze.

"You sound like shit too. Get in my car."

He drops me off. I stagger through the doors marked "Emergency" and inform Big Nurse that I am inches from death. She commands me to take a seat. Is this the last seat I will ever take?

Hours pass. Despite the discomforts of the plastic chairs and having nothing to read but old copies of Us magazine— this is way before cell phones — I'm not feeling half bad when I hear my name called.
They take my vitals.

"You work out a lot, right?"

"Well, I *work* a lot, why?"

"You have the resting pulse rate of a highly trained athlete."

Say it again! Despite my immense beauty, inside I'm

still a lonely, insecure teenager.

They wheel me to what appears to be a parking lot except instead of cars, gurneys. They pull my gurney curtain shut. From my parking spot I can overhear the doctor who'd auscultated me earlier:

"And this patient — Paul Hossfield — move him to the front of the queue. I suspect something serious there."

Something serious! My sphincter peaks at 8.5, minimum. Cancer? Heart disease? I'm too young to die, much less spend the rest of my life dragging around an oxygen tank or some shit!

They wheel me into a little examination room. In comes a new doctor — new to me that is — about my age and amped as fuck.

"You have a collapsed lung. It usually happens to young males who are in good shape. No one knows why."

Before I have time to bask in his evaluation of me as being in good shape, he starts rooting through cabinets as frantically as me searching for my perpetually lost glasses.

"Oh Christ! Where's the pneumothorax kit?" He storms out of the room muttering, "What's with this fucking hospital?" Minutes later, he bursts back through the door carrying a polished wooden box. He snaps open the latches and pulls out a contraption about the size of a severed forearm with a handle sticking out one end and an array of vicious- looking mechanical claws protruding from the other. It looks like an instrument of medieval torture! Sphincter clench 10! He must see my look of horror because he opines, "Oh, don't worry. This part doesn't hurt."

How reassuring.

"OK let's numb you up." He pulls out one of the biggest syringes I'd ever seen and before I could react, buries it between two of my ribs. As a mercy from God, the Novocaine acts almost immediately. Then he whips 'round the aforementioned instrument of torture, jams the clawed end into the numb spot, and begins turning the crank. A series of sickening crunching sounds issues forth but as promised, it doesn't hurt.

When he finishes he attaches a tube to the nice new hole in my chest. The other end is connected to a little bubbling plastic tank attached to my gurney. Then he gets up in my face and asks, "Ever clench your ass really hard when you are holding in a wicked shit? That's called a kegel. Do it for me now." I do it. "Good," he says, "You're going to need that later."

He plunks down on one of those little doctor stools and wheels himself around to face me again. "OK. I'm going to turn this thing on." Wasn't it on already? "No, I mean on. When I do, about 95 percent of the re-inflation of your lung will take place in about 30 seconds to one minute. Most patients find this very distressing. In fact, many say they felt as if they were dying, but don't worry. No one ever dies during this part of it."

Gotta love that bedside manner!

Points for honesty though. He fires that sucker up and **DAMN!** I think I have some idea what waterboarding must be like. They wheel me into the hallway. I tell one of the attendants, "I had to wait so long in the lobby I almost went home," conveniently forgetting I would have had to walk 8 miles on a collapsed lung.

"Oh, that's OK, you would have been back. Dead maybe, but back." Everybody's a comedian.

Chapter 9

Marine Scientists Discover That the Dolphin Clitoris Provides Pleasure : Maybe they could issue a press release on the human clitoris

Carol Lennox

Psychotherapist, Hypnotherapist Sharing new choices.
Leans Left. Mindfulness practitioner before it was cool.
LPC, M.Ed. Helping you make a difference every day.
carollennox.medium.com

Imagine you're a dolphin. One with a penis. As you skip across the water dancing on your fin toward a dolphin with a vagina and clitoris, what's the first thing you need to know?

"How do I make this dolphin feel really good so she lets me put my penis in her vagina?"
Or — if you don't have a penis — "How can I get her to let me rub my clitoris against hers?"

Because making the female of any mammalian species feel good is exactly what gets you laid. Especially the second time.

According to scientists, the dolphin clitoris is chock full of nerves. This is great news for the sleek, savvy suitor. Even more so for the clitoris owner.

It also has an S shape bend allowing it to extend further when aroused. Definitely a design improvement over human clitoris.

Best of all, it's closer to the vagina than the human female's. Their clitoris is positioned in the anterior aspect of the vaginal entrance. It's difficult to have sex with a female dolphin without stimulating her clitoris. Making me wonder if dolphins were the original creations and humans were a second thought. That is if Darwin was wrong and we were created instead of evolving.

If so, why was the Genital Creator in the Sky so generous to dolphins while forcing humans to go on an expedition to first locate and then — we hope — learn to stimulate the clitoris? It was that damned Garden of Eden, wasn't it? Or, if you have a brain to go with your genitalia — and dolphins have bigger brains than humans too — it was evolution.

Floating in salty water is very sensual. The constant flow over clitorises would stimulate the clitoris to grow and expand. The dolphin clitoris likely evolved to allow more surface to connect with ocean waves, as well as other dolphin genitalia.

This is my speculation, not a part of the study. I'm not a marine biologist, but I've swum both naked in the ocean and with dolphins — albeit not at the same time — and therefore have some basis for this idea.

Swim naked in the ocean and find out how good it feels. Just don't try it near a pod of dolphins as they are known to love sex so much they'll try to have it with humans. In fact, when you swim with dolphins and hold onto their flippers while they tow you, you're actually masturbating them, just so you know.

The Toronto Sun reports:
According to one chapter of a 2003 book titled "Marine Mammals: Fisheries, Tourism and Management Issues," researchers observing 29 "lone, sociable dolphins" found that at least 13 dolphins had "periods of misdirected sexual behaviors towards humans, buoys, and/or vessels. . ."

My question, though probably not yours, is who decides these sexual behaviors are misdirected? Do we not all have vaginas, penises, or clitorises? Are dolphins not intelligent, happy-go-lucky floating pleasure palaces? Don't both our species make love year-round, not just during times of ovulation? If you rub us the right way, do we not orgasm? Have none of us looked at a buoy or even a sea-going vessel and wondered, 'What would happen if I rubbed against that?'"

I digress. The point is that evolutionary marine biologists took a deep dive into dolphin clitorises while the human clitoris jumps up-and-down, waving its tiny, rosy arms, trying to get the attention of any scientists.
Yes, the human clitoris has "arms." *
They extend down from the glans and shaft deep into the

vulva. They wrap around the vaginal opening and hug the top of it.

Unfortunately for human clitoris owners, evolution or the Universe decided to place the tip of ours at the top rather than the anterior, move it a few inches above the vaginal opening, and hide most of it "underground." Making ours more difficult to find, much less stimulate. A clear indication that dolphins are the favorites of the Great Genital Creator in the Sky, not humans.
On the other hand, humans have fingers with which to find and stimulate the clitoral head, and to tease and apply pressure along the sides of the vulva and the top of the vaginal opening to stimulate the vast part of the human clitoris that's hidden.

Dolphins have fins and flukes, which are not nearly as flexible as fingers. While they use fins, flukes, and noses to stimulate clitorises, lack of dexterity requires the clitoris be easily accessible in a dolphin. Design or evolution? You decide.

Regardless, humans have more digits to compensate for our smaller brains. Let's use them, shall we? Then there'll be no need to swim with dolphins. Unless that's your kink.

*Not a scientific term

Chapter 10

Please Accept My Friend Request So I Can Make You Regret It : A message from the kid who sat next to you in Spanish twenty-five years ago

Sarah Paris

Author of Signs My Toddler Has a Drinking Problem
(humor collection on Amazon)
Freelance writer of all things. Fiction is my heartbeat.
Believer. Adventurer. Semi-funny.
parissb.medium.com

Hi there! I keep cropping up in your "People You May Know" list, and my name sounds vaguely familiar. You see we have thirty friends in common, and so you finally accept my two-year-old friend request.

You'll find yourself awash in joy as a result.

Thanks for the add! I just scrolled back through all of your social media photos and "loved" them. You're kind of creeped out, as you have fifteen hundred online photos. Don't fret! It just shows how deeply I invest in my online friendships.

You ask your best friend from high school who I am, and she reminds you of our deep and abiding 8th grade Spanish class friendship.

Who you are now

You're now an epidemiologist. You post a well-articulated, thoughtful post imploring all to get vaccinated. You say we're living in unprecedented times. Fake news!

Let's normalize precedented. What does an epidemiologist even do? "Sheeple," I write. I type a 17-paragraph response telling you "more people die from the vaccine" and explain I've done my own research. You're welcome!

When you post photos of your gorgeous family and cute puppy, I won't forget the vaccination post. I'll tie it into all further comments.

"Cute kids," I write. "I hope you're not fear-mongering them into vaccination!"

Until our burgeoning online friendship, our last interaction had consisted of asking each other, "Donde es la playa?"

Man, those were some great times. I feel like you've forgotten the memories we shared, though.

Let me help you remember

Back in 8th grade Spanish, we laughed and bonded. One January day, you asked me how my Winter Break had gone. "Great," I said. You smiled and whispered, "Awesome." Kismet.

I know we can recapture our "que pasa" exuberance. We shared something special! You're brainwashed, but I'll bring you back.

When I share misinformed memes about stolen elections on your page, I'm just trying to recapture our spark. On the last day of 8th grade, I told you to have a great summer. "Gracias," you replied. I daily replay that magical moment in my head.

Yesterday, when you posted a linked article from a medical journal, I wrote:
"Haha. Wrong"

I wanted to point out your erroneous ways as I've watched three videos starring a guy named Dr. Fred. I know he's a real doctor as he wears a stethoscope. You say you went to Johns Hopkins Medical School and did your residency at Harvard? Stop lying, Samantha.

None of your fifteen hundred photos feature you in a lab coat or wearing a stethoscope. Do you want to fill my head with non-researched propaganda? Dr. Fred provides the entire counterattack I need.

Today, I combed through your comments from real-life friends and called each a lying lizard snowflake. I do this because I care so much about you, and I want you to see the light. I won't give up until we are sweetly whispering conjugated Spanish verbs to one another.

Oh no! I see that in your haste to love my comments, you inadvertently hit the block button. Don't worry — neither of us can escape what fate has written in stone. I'll create another profile and send you another friend request. If it would make you happy, I'll create a dozen profiles, so we may rekindle our flames.

I'm so glad you spent so many years waiting for me, too. You must have felt the flickers of hope spark as I insulted your brother and husband in a single comment!

As I wait for you to accept my newest friend requests, I'll make sure to search for you in the threads on mutual friends' pages. I'll let you know you're wrong there, too. I don't know what more I can do to prove my dedication to you. I'm thinking of posting memories from Spanish class for the next three weeks and tagging you.

The time you asked me if you could borrow a pencil and then added a "por favor"? Pure bliss. I think I fell in lifelong love with you that fated day. I see you hovering over accepting a friend request from Brad Dudley, who you think you may have dated for two weeks during your freshman year of college. Alas, Brad is my new alias.

Go ahead and accept it. I think you'll be delighted by the treasure trove of close-up genital photos I have at the ready. I'm so glad we could reconnect.

Chapter 11

I Left My Face Print On The Movie Theater And It Remained There For Five Years : The story of a semi-permanent mark

Sara Zadrima

Writing // Production Coordinating // Art-ing // Probably crying or sweating // she/her // @sarzad on Twitter // @sartzad on IG // MuddyUm Co-Editor
sarazadrima.com/

"**R**UN!"
I heard.
So I *shockingly* did just that.
In fact, I ran face first, smack into the glass wall between two glass doors — even though one of them was propped open by my now laughing little brother whose voice I had blindly obeyed just seconds earlier.

I was in high school, excited to get into the theatre for a midnight premiere of a screen adaptation of one of my favorite book series.

My brother's yell lit the firecracker of excitement inside me, but it was misdirected in a way that launched my face into a sheet of glass.

My automatic tear trigger was activated as my nose was squashed, and I felt the cold drops running down my face as I ricocheted backwards and landed on my butt. I put my hand up to my face to assess the damage and smeared blood and tears across my hand. My nose lit up with pain, but at least it was still attached to my face. I felt a big, deep belly laugh bubble up and erupt through my tears as I collapsed in laughter.

After the big, disorienting smack, I lay on the ground, giggling while tears and blood poured out of my face. I looked up and around me, panning around in slow-mo, and realized everyone else had keeled over with laughter, too.

While I did happen to be in excruciating pain, it was nice to be the source of the full laughter I became enveloped in.

When I tell this story, people usually ask me, "Why and HOW did you manage to miss the door?"

I don't know if this justifies it, but I'll tell you how it happened, nonetheless. I wasn't looking where I was going because I was mid-sentence in a conversation with my friend who was behind me. When my brother declared "RUN!," I cut myself off and instinctually obeyed, but my head remained turned toward my friend. That means I was not realizing 2 crucial things. 1) I was a stride away from the glass, and 2) I was certainly NOT in the path of the propped open doorway.

When I regained my bearings and breath, our cackles slowed to giggles, and I reached my hands up to my face once more to see if my nose was still firmly attached to my face. Then I got up.

It was pretty bloody and painful — I had smacked it so hard that the skin on the bridge of my nose split open. But I wasn't going to miss this premiere.

My mom suggested a trip to the ER, but I refused. She thought I was stubborn, but I thought I was cool and tough.

That is, until I had to walk past the snaking queue of friends, high school acquaintances, and my CRUSH* in order to get to the snack counter, explain the situation, and obtain a latex glove full of ice for my face only to go right back past the same line of people to regain my spot. *said crush is my current fiancé, so that part worked in my favor.

I had to get up to refill my ice glove periodically throughout the showing, but 16 year old me definitely thought it was worth it.

I learned some important things about myself that day: one being that I could laugh at my own expense, and the other being that I loved making people laugh, even if it involved me getting injured.

The icing on top of the cake though is when I realized that I left my face print on the glass when I went back for another movie several weeks later.

My friends turned it into a game, sending photos of the movie theater window every time they went to see a movie. This lasted almost 5 years, because the movie theater either never cleaned their glass doors, or intentionally left the face print there to honor my legacy. Even though my physical mark on the theater eventually faded, I always have the story in my arsenal of embarrassing/weirdly acquired injuries — which also happens to be the only way I have ever been seriously injured.

Chapter 12

I'm Teaching My 12-Year-Old Son About Women : Calm down!!!!

Amy Sea aka Amy Culberg

16 X Top Writer, Editor— Comedian, Satirist, Humorist, Top Writer. Follow my pub.
Publisher of "Breast Stories" medium.com/boobs-breasts-and-mammaries and
"Amy's World" https://aculberg007.medium.com/

When my grandma was living, I never wrote anything with the word fuck in it. I never ranted anywhere but in my diary and even then, I made sure no one was reading over my shoulder. Being a girl meant you were calm, cool, and collected. I have a son and I want him to understand women are real people, not composites of what other people want them to be. I asked my son what he wanted to know about women. He said he learned all about sex in school, mom.

I was relieved. I dreaded teaching my son about sex. It was only yesterday he stopped nursing. I know 12 is old, but we saved a lot on food and beverages so calm down.

As a son-mother, I am more concerned about him understanding a woman's emotional needs. I asked him to sit down on a chair of nails and hot coals while I explained women to him. I needed his full attention. "The worst thing you can say to a woman," I told him, "is to calm down."

"What about shut the fuck up?" my son asked.

"What about it?" I asked.

"Is that worse or better than calm down?"

"Calm down is always the worst," I said. "Anything you say to a girl is better than calm down."

My son preceded to go down a list of insults. Since none of them contained stupid whore, or the C-word, I kept shaking my head.

"Nope, son," I said. "Calm down is always the worst."

"Why is calm down such a big deal, mom?" he asked. I could feel the limbic system of my brain swelling. Even the words calm down in a sentence, in any order, made me want to punch a hole through the wall.

"It just is," I said, causing my blood to boil so hot, I tipped my ear, poured out the hot blood, added some chamomile, and made some soothing tea to calm my nerves.

"Dad," my son said, turning to his father. "Why is calm down the worst thing you can say to a woman?"

My husband shook his head. "It just makes them really mad," my husband said.

Even the two of them discussing it made me wonder where I'd put my knives.

"But mom," my son said. "I don't get it. Why?"

"That's it!" I said. "I'm going to bed." I had to get out of there before I started ripping the baseboards off the floors.

"But what about the family movie?" My son asked all innocently like he hadn't been baiting me like a goddamn salmon.

"Not tonight," I said. "Just let me leave." I grabbed onto the wall to hold myself steady.

"Mom," my son said. "Calm down."

I know you think I lost my cool when my son said this. You probably think I blew up, ripped the copper pipes from my walls, and set my living room on fire. You might have imagined I crashed my dining room chairs over my knees and shot multiple holes through my big screen tv, but you'd be wrong.
I don't have copper pipes.

ele

Chapter 13

Science Abandons Red Counties "Just not worth the crap we take from pseudoscience," say Physics and Chemistry

Andrew Rodwin

MuddyUm co-editor. Top writer in Humor and Satire per some esoteric algorithm designed by Medium alchemists. Also yoga, rowing, reading, hanging with my golden. andrew-rodwin.medium.com

Red county residents are preparing for possible changes in the laws of the Universe by stocking up on canned food, hydroxychloroquine, and ammunition.

Science announced it's withdrawing from all red counties, effective June 1. Shares in Merck (MRK), manufacturer of ivermectin, rose 62% on the news. Rumors predicting Science's exit have been circulating since last April when Law became the first major discipline to withdraw from red counties. After the terror attack on the Capitol, and the unwillingness of Republicans to recognize the perpetrators as criminals, Law decided it could no longer operate effectively where people regarded it as some sort of opt-in freemium upgrade.

According to a Science spokesperson, the grace period is intended to give red counties time to choose how the world will function in the absence of Science. *"Pseudoscience has some big decisions to make. Will gravity remain the result of massive objects warping the curvature of space time? Or is it assumed God rewards you for not skipping church by holding down the Jalepeno Poutine Mini Donut Bowl [1] on your snack tray with his index finger while you watch reruns of Duck Dynasty? Keep evolution? Or maybe God created ebola and head lice just to remind humanists who calls the shots."*

Asked whether Science believed red counties could effectively manage life without science, the spokesperson sighed.

"Honestly? Who gives a shit? Science has bestowed the benefits of thousands of years of thorough research, painstaking investigation, personal sacrifice, and creative genius on the GOP. They take it for granted — as long as Discovery Channel doesn't preempt Nascar — and whine whenever Science tells them something inconvenient. Like California's wildfires were caused by 'unusual drought and heat exacerbated by climate change.'[12] Not Jewish space lasers."

---

[1] pressreader.com/canada/the-province/20150630/282428462842424
[2] earthobservatory.nasa.gov/images/148908/whats-behind-californias-surge-of-large-fires

Asked whether Science would reconsider, the spokesperson grimaced.

"Galileo was persecuted for advocating heliocentrism, which everyone now accepts. Well, everyone except Marjorie Taylor Greene, but Science hasn't yet proved she's not a collective hallucination. The null hypothesis. Fingers crossed, data looks good. Anyway, we've had enough of our best people, like Dr. Fauci, getting Galileo'ed by mobs of ignorant yahoos. Stick a fork in it. Done."

Medicine, a branch of Science, will also withdraw. In its absence, renowned healers like Joe Rogan, Rand Paul, and Dr. Phil will have an opportunity to don surgical gowns and demonstrate how true patriots insert stents and excise tumors. Rogan said it was time for big changes anyway.

"Why stents? Let's use crazy straws! Just bought a warehouse full of them. Gonna make a killing. OK, I might rephrase. So that's off the record, asshole."

Mitch McConnell (R-KY) dismissed the withdrawal of Science as a "Democratic publicity stunt by a bunch of wolf-crying left-wing crackpots, like the Union of Concerned Scientists."

Added McConnell,
"America's primary mission is restoring me to Mount Olympus, to rejoin Apollo and Demeter, so I don't waste more time listening to a bunch of shovel-toting miners

back home gripe about black lung. So what if we have to reinvent chemistry. Let's focus on what's fundamental to the nation's survival. Preserving the filibuster."

Governor Greg Gianforte (R-MT) chimed in. *"We're tired of Science whining about how we treated Galileo, another ivory-tower liberal Democrat tone deaf to American patriots."*

When a Times reporter pointed out that Galileo was an Italian born in the 16th century and is regarded as the father of modern physics, Gianforte responded with his trademark debating tactic, body-slamming the newswoman to the floor.

As a result, Journalism attended a summit with History, Mathematics, and other disciplines to decide whether to follow Science's lead and withdraw all presence from red counties.

- Math said they have the votes to jointly withdraw, per complex formulae no one else understands.
- History claimed the meeting would long be remembered, "much like the Yalta Conference, except without a придурок like Stalin."
- Logic, ever the wag, quipped they may add more disciplines via Monotonicity of entailment. [3]

---

[3] en.wikipedia.org/wiki/Monotonicity_of_entailment

Donald Trump dismissed concerns about whether the withdrawal of Science posed a risk to people in his base, who might irrevocably metamorphose into dark energy when the fundamental laws of the Universe cease to apply.

"Astronomology? Chemics? Biogonomy? None of them voted for me. Not a fan. Well, except for Dr. Oz. He's OK for a guy with a prayer rug. We'll build a wall to keep the scientists out. I've got armies of pseudoscientists. Why do I need scientists?"

Anyway, Rudy's got a degree in Crimino, Crimics, umm, Criminometrics. I've already asked him to run NASA. So we're good.

"Can I still get a Triple Whopper with Cheese?"

Chapter 14

On Learning to Speak American: How many ways can you say hot cocoa?

Lucia Siochi

Artist at heart, Technologist by trade. Lover of cats and coffee, life, and laughter. Sharing my quirky point-of-view.
Twitter: @LuciaSioch. luciasiochi.medium.com

I never had an accent until I arrived in the U.S. I got on a plane, and several flights later, BAM! I had an accent.

I grew up in another country and spoke much like everyone else around me. We sounded similar to each other. Then I moved to the States, and suddenly I sounded different from everyone else.

Although I grew up overseas, English was my native tongue. We spoke English at home and had English classes every year in school. Most of our classes and textbooks were in English, not just our English classes. I read American books voraciously. We watched American television shows and listened to American music. Now that I think about it, I suppose we lived much like American ex-pats!

We used words from American English instead of British English. For example, we say elevator instead of lift.

The point of all this is I thought I already 'spoke American.' Then I discovered that the most effective way to learn how to 'speak American' is to live in the United States and actually talk to Americans.

Even though I used the same words Americans did, I still had to adjust my accent to minimize confusing the locals and streamline my interactions with them.
I also wanted to blend in and avoid getting this:
You ain't from 'round here, are ya?

Most people were patient and accommodating, though. Also, the population then was not as diverse as it is now, so I suppose they could clearly see that I didn't look like I was from around there!

Hot Cocoa

I still remember one of my early linguistic mishaps. At a snack bar, I wanted some Hot Cocoa. That's what was written on the menu up on the wall behind the counter. So that's what I asked for. I pronounced it as: hot ko-KO-wa.

The lady behind the counter looked confused, so I pointed to the menu. She read out loud: hot KO-ko. Then she exclaimed, "Oh, you mean hot chocolate!"

Apparently, here in the States, the 'a' in 'cocoa' is silent. Worse yet, apparently 'cocoa' is pronounced 'chocolate.' I didn't argue with her. I just wanted my hot whatever-you-call-it.

Broccoli

It didn't take long for me to pick up the local accent. But now and then, I'd say a word 'the wrong way.' I'd make a mental note of the 'proper' pronunciation and practice saying it that way until it became automatic. One such word is broccoli. This is how I said it when I first got here in the States: broh-KO-lee. This is how I relearned to say it: BROK-lee, similar to 'rock.'

If I'd never seen or heard this word before and didn't know what it meant, this is how I would spell it based on the local pronunciation: 'brockly.' The second 'o' in broccoli is silent.

Millimeter

Now that I've lived here in the States for decades, you'd assume my American accent should be flawless. For the most part, it is. Though I still have to pause and think before saying the word millimeter.

I hurriedly debate with myself in my head whether to say it this way: mi-LI- mi-tr, similar to saying 'limiter.' Or this way: MI-lee-MEE-tr, similar to saying 'milly meter.' I go through a similar process with the word 'centimeter.'

These two words don't naturally come up in conversation, so I don't get much practice saying them. Perhaps I should interject them randomly into sentences more often. Then I'll have them down pat!

After picking up an American accent, you might think I've lost my original accent. Nope. I've got both now. Which one I use depends on who I'm talking to.

When I'm around Americans, I speak with my American accent. When I'm around my relatives or grade school classmates, I speak with my original accent. I don't think about it — I automatically switch accents, like a chameleon instinctively blending in. The best part is whoever I talk to doesn't think I have an accent because I speak like them. So, nope, I don't have an accent anymore. Again.

Just don't ask me to give you any small measurements in metric!

Chapter 15

My Neighbor Saw My Bare Butt: And unfortunately, I saw his peanuts

Rachael Ann Sand

Passionate about the next generation of all living things. Sharing life lessons & experiences with humor and love. rachaelannsand.medium.com

66 "Auntie Rachie, girls have vaginas and boys have peanuts!" My toddler-age niece proudly proclaimed her newfound knowledge as I walked in. Surprised and amused, I wasn't prepared to offer pronunciation lessons. While we're on the topic of private parts, I'll refer to my niece as Junebug, for privacy purposes.

When Junebug witnessed Mommy changing an infant boy's diaper, her insatiable toddler curiosity led to a conversation every parent looks forward to — Anatomy 101. Mommy told her the 'proper' names. When Junebug so confidently translated penis to peanuts the adults found it so endearing we didn't correct her.

My first glimpse of a boy's anatomy was likely in the bathtub with one of my brothers. I imagine they're thankful I have no memory of it. I do remember my most embarrassing childhood nudity encounter. I didn't intend to go public with my story. However, when MuddyUm

published the butt humor prompt I realized there is no age limit to an audience for ass-centric humor.
Fart, toot, poop, penis, boobs, ass, butt, dick, derrière— these words have an undeniable power to produce giggles and smirks at any age. They also have the power to get a person slapped in the face. It's all about context. Humorists play with toeing the line. Sometimes we misstep and fall on our ass, sometimes we are the butt of our own joke. It's all comedy.

On the day of the incident, I was playing outside with a neighbor boy. Let's call him Norbert. If he runs for president, applies to adopt a child, or attempts to join the CIA, I'd hate to be the one who revealed a skeleton in his closet. Publicizing the story of Norbert flashing his peanuts at a young girl — that's not the kind of scandal I want to be famous for.

At the time, I had conquered potty training yet still lacked mature body awareness. Completely engrossed in sandbox shenanigans, I suddenly realized my bladder had reached a critical point. Sprinting to my front door and nearly tripping down the stairs, I desperately yanked down my bottoms and landed on the toilet seat just in time.

My relief was quickly replaced by the shock of realizing I'd been followed. Norbert was not only witnessing me pee — he was whipping out his peanuts! It happened so fast all I could do was scream helplessly as he peed on my lap. Technically he was aiming at the toilet, but the seat was occupied. I couldn't jump up because my own stream was still flowing. In reality, it was over quickly but I felt as though I'd been trapped on that toilet for ages, held captive by bodily functions. Although we had both made it to the bathroom, one of us still ended up covered in pee. Wasn't the point of potty training to avoid that?

In retrospect, squatting in the sandbox like a cat in a litter box may have been more sanitary. If Norbert was going to see my bare butt, at least we could have avoided the pissing contest. All my post-potty training life I've envied a clear advantage of male anatomy — the ease at which they can pee outside. If Norbert had done me the courtesy of peeing on a tree instead of on me, he would've spared me the em-bare-ass-ment of an awkward encounter.

Authors

About MuddyUm

Wouldn't You Rather Be Laughing?

MuddyUm[4] is a growing non-profit humor publication hosted on the Medium blogging platform. Our mission is to bring all forms of humor to the world, by providing a platform for a globally diverse community of humor and comedy writers, cartoonists, and readers to share stories. We publish for the love of it, to make the world a better place.

As of July 2022, In addition to our Founder and Editor-in-Chief, Susan Brearley, we have 13 volunteer editors, three interns, and nearly 900 contributing writers. We averaged more than 40 published stories each week, with over 18,000 reads weekly, and millions of loyal fans.

We also have an active internship program[5] where college students interested in humor, publishing, and social media help our editors with social media strategy and posts, and learn the art of writing crisp, punchy prose.

MuddyUm actively posts humorous content on Medium, Facebook, Twitter, TikTok, YouTube, and Instagram.

---

[4] medium.com/muddyum
[5] available to all colleges on Handshake

MuddyUm periodically hosts a comedy camp [6]where renowned humorists teach workshops on writing and performing comedy.

To join the MuddyUm community as a writer or editor, please send us an email introducing yourself.

Captain@muddyum.org

---

[6] MuddyUm.org

Zazzle, Newsletter & Social Media handles

ZAZZLE

Show your support of MuddyUm Pirates and Outlaws by grabbing the swag on the MuddyUm Zazzle Storefront. Enjoy custom artwork on coffee mugs and t-shirts, useful things when sailing the high seas of humor, and need a clean shirt and a cup of tea to release the Comedy Kraken!

Purchases support MuddyUm editors, writers, artists, anthology projects, and the occasional return ticket from Uranus.
zazzle.com/mbr/238390904454564145

Newsletter

If you like this kind of thing, you will love more of this kind of thing! Sign up for the MuddyUm Newsletter and receive a weekly collection of TEN stories curated to tickle the finely tuned, critical laugh theory machine that is your twisted mind. You want ten funny stories about forest creatures? We got that. You want ten funny stories about your grandmother? We got that. You want ten funny stories about butts? We have FORTY funny stories about butts! Sign up for the MuddyUm newsletter. All you have to lose is your dignity and self-respect.

To subscribe, click the "Subscribe" button below any MuddyUm Medium article.
Follow MuddyUm on: Medium, Instagram, YouTube, Twitter, TikTok and Facebook Via our Social Media Portal
Social Media Portal: muddyum.carrd.co/

About The Founder

Susan Brearley

Susan Brearley was found in a basket on the Nile river floating among the reeds. Egypt at the time was going through kind of a slump—all the plagues, frogs, and first-born dying. But when Pharaoh saw Susan's infant face, he broke out in peals of laughter. This event marked the beginning of the important, but poorly understood, "Running with Satire Dynasty" (2500 BCE to Last Thursday). God, however, hardened Pharaoh's heart so that he would hoard all the funny for himself. Finally, Susan stood up to Pharaoh and said, "Let my people laugh!"

Susan struck out that night across the land, carrying her message of funny to Canaan, Syria, Moscow, the Hague, Slough, and, finally, Poughkeepsie. The story of her travels was made into a "road movie" with Bernadette Peters playing Susan, and Tim Curry as Marty Feldman—whose unrequited love for Susan set Hollywood ablaze in scandal. From her aerie in mid-State New York, Susan founded and edits MuddyUm and untold multitudes of other publications, while also continuing experiments to re-animate the lifeless corpses of criminally insane prisoners buried in Potter's Field.

Because of her background, Susan wants to support funny writers in the worst way (which is in a hammock with high heels) and provide a publication that will support writers through editing, publication, and promotion.

The MuddyUm tagline—the title of this book—came to Susan when she was approached by missionaries one Saturday, and they explained about Revelations and the peril that hovered over Susan's soul, like a hummingbird with a space laser. "Let me see if I've got this straight," said Susan. "One-third of the seas will turn to blood, and one-third of the fishes will die. But is that one-third of the fishes left after the seas turn to blood? Because if one-third of the seas turn to blood, that will automatically kill one-third of all fishes. Which—hurray for God, two fishes, one stone—but if a third of the remaining fish are also killed, that just seems spiteful. Anyway, what have the fishes ever done to God?"

The missionaries sputtered about whether or not her soul would be redeemed.

"See," she said, "I have problems with the model of SOUL as COMMODITY. If a soul can be 'redeemed,' can it be banked against future earnings, is it fungible, or even non-fungible?"

The missionaries told Susan, "You need to get right with God!"

"I think I'd rather be laughing," she said. "Wouldn't you rather be laughing?"

Also By

Gary Chapin
126 Falsehoods We Believe About Education
available on Lulu,com

Toni Crowe
NEVER A $7 WH*RE: It Doesn't Matter Where You
Started available on Amazon
Bullets And Bosses Don't Have Friends available on
Amazon

Anu Anniah
Mommy's 'Lectures' To Kanda available on Amazon
Eye Am In Denial: And other funny stories available on
Amazon

Susan Brearley
A Safe and Brave Space Anthology of Poetry and Art
Available on Lulu;
Battlefield Hope available on Amazon

Sarah Paris
Signs My Toddler Has a Drinking Problem: and other
humorous stories available on Amazon

www.ingramcontent.com/pod-product-compliance
Lightning Source LLC
LaVergne TN
LVHW051814080426
835513LV00017B/1952